EXPLORING BIOMES
DESERT BIOMES

by Lela Nargi

Ideas for Parents and Teachers

Pogo Books let children practice reading informational text while introducing them to nonfiction features such as headings, labels, sidebars, maps, and diagrams, as well as a table of contents, glossary, and index.

Carefully leveled text with a strong photo match offers early fluent readers the support they need to succeed.

Before Reading

- "Walk" through the book and point out the various nonfiction features. Ask the student what purpose each feature serves.
- Look at the glossary together. Read and discuss the words.

Read the Book

- Have the child read the book independently.
- Invite him or her to list questions that arise from reading.

After Reading

- Discuss the child's questions. Talk about how he or she might find answers to those questions.
- Prompt the child to think more. Ask: Deserts have many animals and plants. How have they adapted to living in this biome?

Pogo Books are published by Jump!
5357 Penn Avenue South
Minneapolis, MN 55419
www.jumplibrary.com

Library of Congress Cataloging-in-Publication Data

Names: Nargi, Lela, author.
Title: Desert biomes / by Lela Nargi.
Description: Pogo books. | Minneapolis, MN: Jump!, Inc., [2023] | Series: Exploring biomes | Includes index.
Audience: Ages 7-10
Identifiers: LCCN 2021053213 (print)
LCCN 2021053214 (ebook)
ISBN 9781636907505 (hardcover)
ISBN 9781636907512 (paperback)
ISBN 9781636907529 (ebook)
Subjects: LCSH: Desert ecology–Juvenile literature.
Classification: LCC QH541.5.D4 N34 2022 (print)
LCC QH541.5.D4 (ebook)
DDC 577.54–dc23/eng/20211028
LC record available at
https://lccn.loc.gov/2021053213
LC ebook record available at
https://lccn.loc.gov/2021053214

Editor: Eliza Leahy
Designer: Emma Bersie

Photo Credits: Jon Manjeot/Shutterstock, cover (left); Armin Rose/Shutterstock, cover (right); LHBLLC/Shutterstock, 1; Eric Isselee/Shutterstock, 3; Bildagentur Zoonar GmbH/Shutterstock, 4; imageBROKER/Alamy, 5; Giusparta/Shutterstock, 6-7t; Andrelix/Shutterstock, 6-7b; Max Novick/Shutterstock, 8; Buiten-Beeld/Alamy, 9; Cristina Lichti/Alamy, 10-11; Rick & Nora Bowers/Alamy, 12-13; CORREIA Patrice/Alamy, 14-15; Andrius Zigmantas/Dreamstime, 16-17t; Patrick Poendl/Shutterstock, 16-17b; Songquan Deng/Shutterstock, 18; PhotoStock-Israel/Alamy, 19; Tavarius/Shutterstock, 20-21; Anan Kaewkhammul/Shutterstock, 23.

Printed in the United States of America at Corporate Graphics in North Mankato, Minnesota.

TABLE OF CONTENTS

CHAPTER 1

· ·

ALWAYS DRY

Why is it so dry in the Kalahari? It is a desert **biome**! Like most deserts, the Kalahari in southern Africa is very dry. It gets less than 10 inches (25 centimeters) of **precipitation** each year.

Kalahari Desert

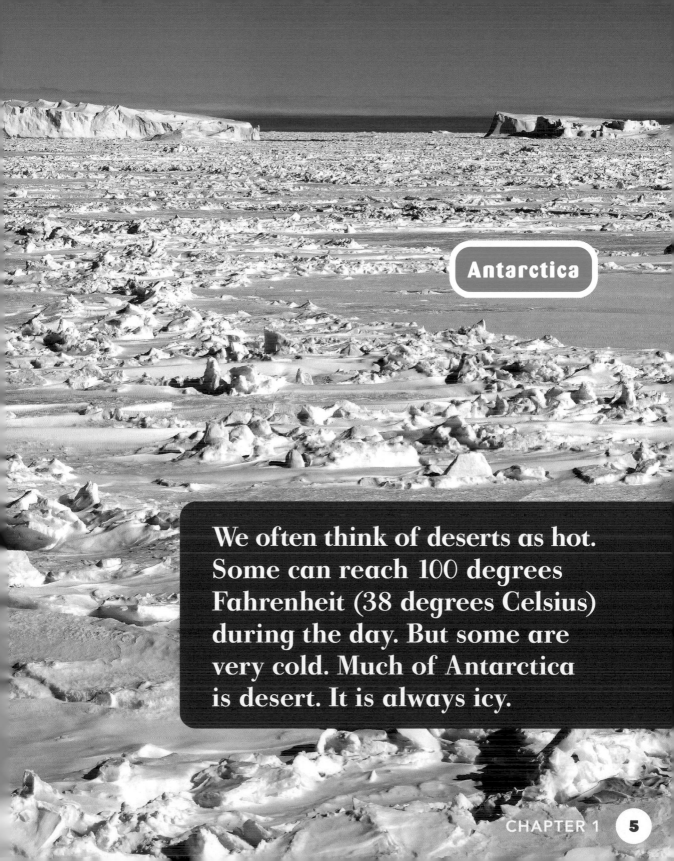

Antarctica

We often think of deserts as hot. Some can reach 100 degrees Fahrenheit (38 degrees Celsius) during the day. But some are very cold. Much of Antarctica is desert. It is always icy.

Turpan Depression

Deserts like the Kalahari are sandy. Others are not. China's Turpan Depression is rocky. It is surrounded by mountains.

Death Valley in California has salt flats. These form when salt water **evaporates**. It leaves behind a layer of salt.

Death Valley

TAKE A LOOK!

Deserts make up 20 percent of Earth's land. Take a look!

■ = desert

CHAPTER 2

FULL OF LIFE

Water is hard to find in deserts. But many plants and animals live here. They have **adapted** to dryness. Some desert plants get **moisture** from **dew**.

dew

fog

Atacama Desert in Chile is on the coast. Here, plants get moisture from **fog**.

thorn

Desert plants grow far apart.
They have wide root systems.
Roots grow deep in the
ground. These are all
ways the plants get water.

Mesquite trees have deep
roots. They are also covered
in thorns. This protects them
from hungry animals.

Many plants lose water through tiny **pores** in their leaves. A cactus has no leaves. This helps it store water. Other **succulents** have thick, waxy leaves to keep water in.

Some flowers only open when the sun goes down. Bats, moths, and some bees also like cool times of day. They visit these flowers to eat in the dark.

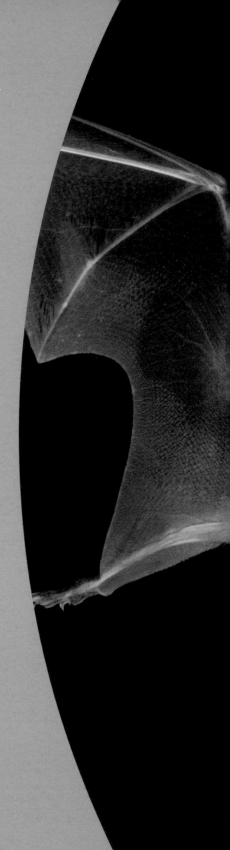

DID YOU KNOW?

Cacti can be spongy or empty inside. A saguaro cactus can hold 1,500 gallons (5,678 liters) of water. That is how much water you drink in eight years!

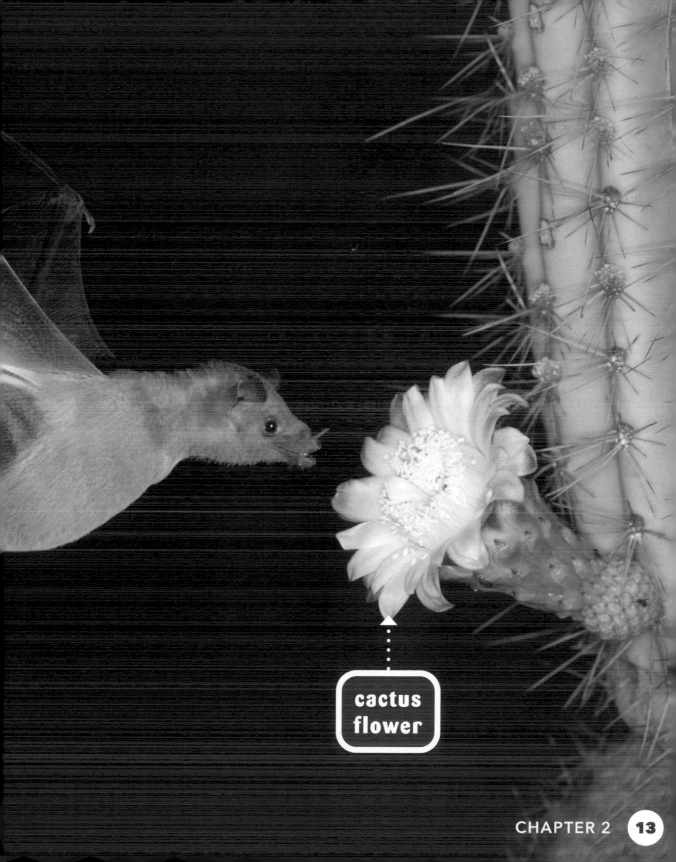

cactus flower

How do animals survive in deserts? Some are active at night, when it is cooler. Cape ground squirrels use their bushy tails as shade. Snakes dig in the sand to get cool. Camels store fat and water in their humps.

Cape ground squirrel

TAKE A LOOK!

Many animals have adapted to live in deserts. Take a look!

CAMEL
stores fat and
water in humps

**CAPE GROUND
SQUIRREL**
uses its tail as shade

COYOTE
digs dens in sand

MEERKAT
closes its ears
to keep out sand

RATTLESNAKE
digs in sand

**WHITE-LINED
SPHINX MOTH**
is active at night

Deserts are full of surprises. A mirage tricks us into seeing water. This happens when hot air bends light.

An oasis is no trick. Water collects from a **spring**. Animals visit for a drink. Fig, olive, and lemon trees might grow nearby.

mirage

oasis

CHAPTER 3

....

DESERTS AND US

One billion people live in desert biomes.
Many cities are located in deserts.
Las Vegas, Nevada, is one.

Las Vegas

quartz

People **mine** in the desert. **Minerals** and gems, such as opal, quartz, and jade, are found here.

Sahara
Desert

Climate change is changing deserts. As Earth heats up and dries out, deserts are growing. When more land turns to desert, forest and grassland biomes disappear.

You can help! How? **Recycle** when you can. Try to use less water. This will help keep Earth's biomes healthy!

DID YOU KNOW?

The Sahara Desert is in North Africa. It has grown 10 percent since 1920.

ACTIVITIES & TOOLS

CACTUS WATER STORAGE

Cacti store water to survive in deserts. See how it works with this fun activity!

What You Need:

- two sponges of the same size and shape
- scissors
- measuring cup
- two cups or glasses
- cookie sheet
- wax paper

① With an adult's help, cut the sponges into cactus shapes.

② Measure ¼ cup of water. Pour it into one glass. Repeat and pour ¼ cup of water into the second glass.

③ Place one sponge in each glass.

④ Wait one hour. Then remove them. How much water did each sponge soak up?

⑤ Place both wet sponges on a cookie sheet.

⑥ Cover one sponge with wax paper. Leave the other sponge uncovered.

⑦ Leave them sitting for two or three days. Which sponge dried out more? Why do you think that is?

GLOSSARY

adapted: Changed to make it easier to live in a certain habitat.

biome: A habitat and everything that lives in it.

climate change: Changes in Earth's weather and climate over time.

dew: Moisture in the form of small drops that collect overnight on cool surfaces outside.

evaporates: Changes into a vapor or gas.

fog: A cloud of mist near the ground.

mine: To dig up minerals that are in the ground.

minerals: Solid substances found in the earth that do not come from animals or plants.

moisture: Wetness, as from rain, snow, dew, or fog.

pores: Tiny holes on the surfaces of plants.

precipitation: The falling of water from the sky in the form of rain, sleet, hail, or snow.

recycle: To process old items such as glass, plastic, newspapers, and aluminum so they can be used to make new products.

spring: A place where water rises to the surface from an underground source.

succulents: Plants that have thick, fleshy leaves for storing moisture.

INDEX

TO LEARN MORE

Finding more information is as easy as 1, 2, 3.

① **Go to www.factsurfer.com**

② **Enter "desertbiomes" into the search box.**

③ **Choose your book to see a list of websites.**

FACT SURFER